A
CHILD'S
BOOK OF
ANIMALS

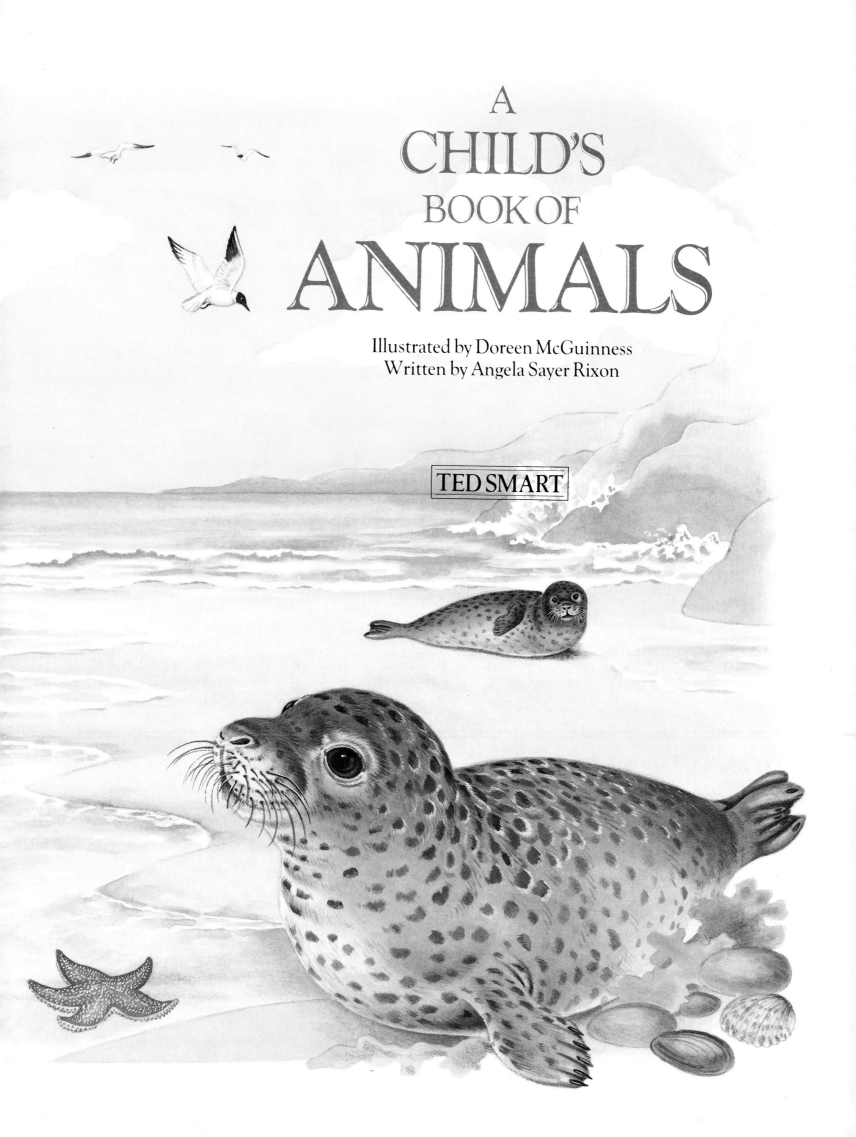

A CHILD'S BOOK OF ANIMALS

Illustrated by Doreen McGuinness
Written by Angela Sayer Rixon

TED SMART

This edition first published in 1991 for The Book People,
Guardian House, Borough Road, Godalming, Surrey GU7 2AE by
Hamlyn Children's Books, part of Reed International Books Ltd.,
Michelin House, 81 Fulham Road, London SW3 6RB

Text copyright © 1990 The Octopus Publishing Group Limited
Illustrations copyright © 1990 by Doreen McGuinness
Doreen McGuinness is represented by Garden Studio, London

ISBN 1-85613-043-6

Printed in Hong Kong

CONTENTS

THE WORLD OF ANIMALS

In this book there are pictures of more than 100 different animals. Some live in hot deserts, some in cold forests, some in high mountains and some just share our houses as pets. On half of the pages, you will see pictures of lots of animals with their names. On the other half, you will be able to read more about how some of these animals live – what they eat, where they build their homes, how they look after their babies.

We hope you enjoy finding out about the exciting world of animals!

Animals in our homes

cat

guinea pig

rabbit

goldfish

budgerigar

dog

9

Pets and their babies

Baby cats are called kittens. They are born with their eyes closed, but after about a week they open them.

10

Mother rabbits make soft nests of hay and fur for their babies. The babies are born without any fur and with their eyes closed. As they grow older, fur grows on their bodies and their eyes open.

Baby dogs are called puppies. Their mother looks after them while they are young. She feeds them with her milk and licks them clean with her wet tongue.

Animals of the seashores

seal

starfish

gull

plover

sea anemone

prawn

crab

Hiding

Crabs live on the beach. Gulls sometimes try to eat them, so they have to hide. Some crabs hide under the rocks in rock pools. Other crabs hide among pieces of seaweed.

Some prawns hide by changing their colour. If they are on the sand, they turn brown. If they are near seaweed or other plants, they turn red or green. At night they turn blue.

Plovers lay their eggs in nests on the seashore. The eggs are grey with brown spots. They look like stones, so other animals do not notice them.

Animals of ponds and rivers

kingfisher

coot

otter

water vole

heron

beaver

salmon

dragonfly

newt

17

Building a home

Beavers have large, strong teeth. They use them to gnaw through tree trunks. They use the tree trunks to build dams across rivers. Behind the dams, the beavers make large nests of sticks, stones and mud, called lodges.

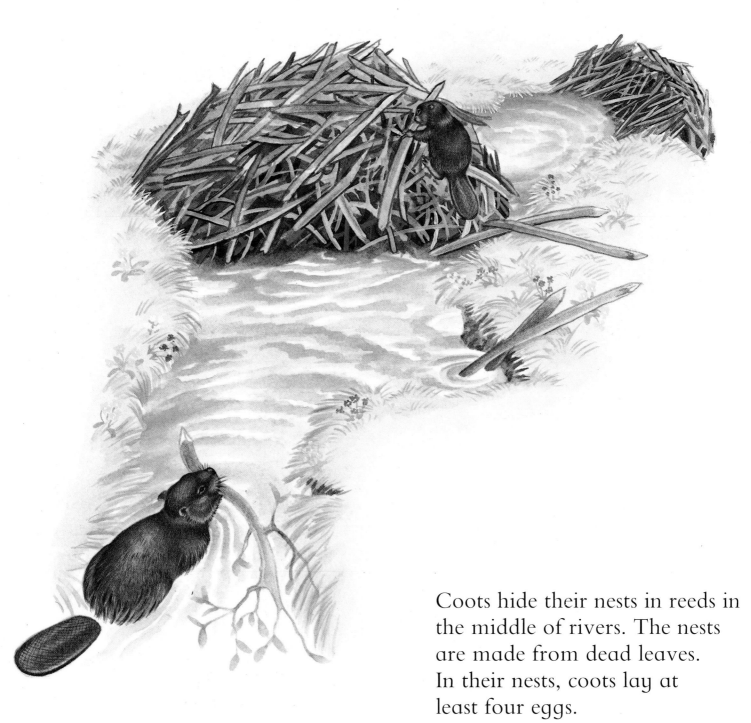

Coots hide their nests in reeds in the middle of rivers. The nests are made from dead leaves. In their nests, coots lay at least four eggs.

Water voles build their homes in river banks.
First they make a hole in the bank, then they
dig long tunnels through the earth. In the
middle of the tunnels, the voles make nests
lined with grass.

Animals of fields and hedgerows

pheasant

hare

mole

adder

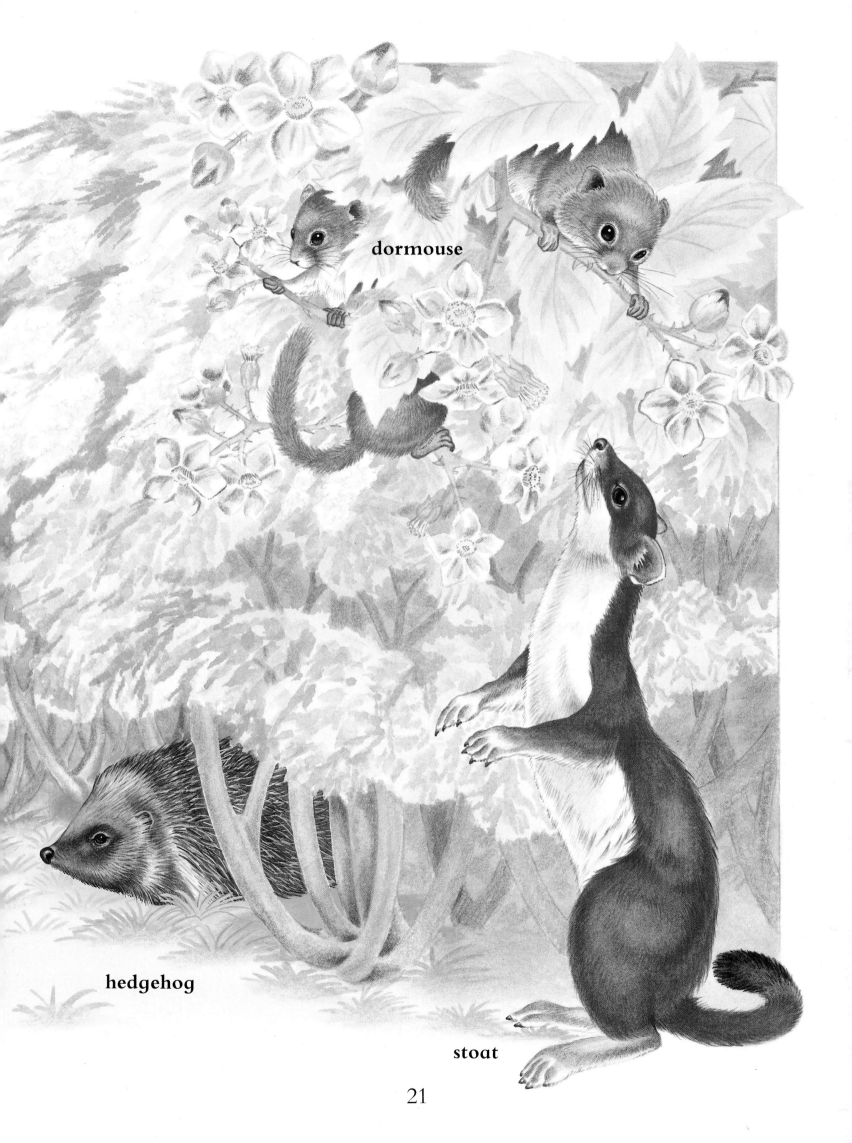

dormouse

hedgehog

stoat

21

Sleeping through the winter

The hedgehog eats slugs, snails and insects.
These are hard to find in the winter. So,
when the cold weather starts, the hedgehog
makes a warm, cosy bed of dry leaves.
It crawls into the bed and curls up into a
tight ball. Then it sleeps until the weather
gets warm again.

The dormouse is another little animal
which sleeps through the winter.
It builds itself a nest with dry leaves
and strips of bark. Then it wraps its
tail around its body and goes to
sleep until spring.

When the cold weather comes, the adder finds a deep,
warm hole. It crawls inside and coils itself round and round.
When it wakes up in the spring, it shakes off its old skin.
Underneath it has a shiny new skin.

Animals on the farm

cow

sheep

pig

chicken

horse

turkey

duck

Farm animals which help us

Many farm animals help us.

Cows give us milk. The farmer milks them with a machine.
Later, a lorry takes the milk to a dairy. There, some milk is
made into butter and cheese. The rest is put into bottles
or cartons for people to buy.

Chickens give us eggs. Each chicken lays an egg every day. The farmer collects the eggs and keeps some for his family. The other eggs are packed into boxes and sent to shops.

Sheep give us wool. They grow thick coats of wool to keep warm in the winter. When the spring comes, the farmer cuts off the thick wool. This is called shearing. The wool is taken to a factory. There it is washed, spun and dyed many bright colours.

Animals of the deep seas

whale

ray

eel

dolphin

shark

sea horse

turtle

octopus

coral

29

Sea animals in danger

Dolphins are small whales. They live in large groups called schools. Dolphins are very clever animals and can be trained to do tricks.

Whales live in the sea, but they breathe air just like people. They can dive under water and stay there for about an hour. Then they must come up to the top to get air again.

Tiny coral animals live together in large groups under the sea. There they grow hard shells around themselves which join up to make reefs. The shells grow in many beautiful colours.

There are not many of these animals left in the world. Now people are trying to protect them so that they do not die out altogether.

31

Animals of ice and snow

polar bear

musk ox

arctic fox

arctic hare

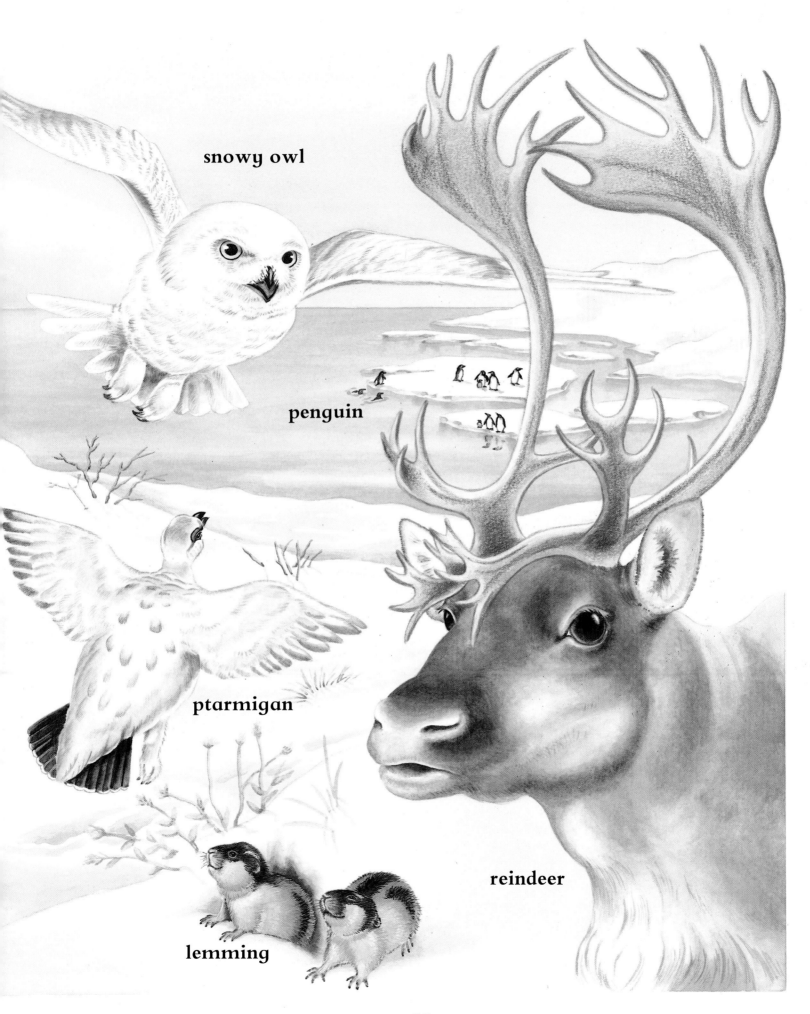

snowy owl

penguin

ptarmigan

lemming

reindeer

33

On the move

Reindeer live in ice and snow for most of the year. They have special feet which help them walk on snow and dig up plants to eat. In the winter, reindeer go on a long journey to warmer places. There they can still find food. They go back to the snow in the spring.

Lemmings are small, furry animals a bit like mice. They make their homes in tunnels under the snow, but they do not always stay there. Sometimes they leave because they need to find food. Sometimes they leave because they have so many babies that there is not enough room for them all.

Musk oxen also live in the snow. They have a thick coat of long hair to keep them warm. When the winter comes, they join together in large groups called herds.
Then, like the reindeer, they walk a very long way to places where they can still find grass and plants to eat.

Animals of the mountains

condor

cougar

llama

red panda

ibex

giant panda

yak

Pandas

Two rare animals live in the mountains of China.
They are both types of panda, but they look quite
different from one another.

The red panda is sometimes called a cat-bear,
because it looks rather like a cat. It spends most
of the day in trees, but climbs down at night
and eats fruit, leaves, seeds and birds' eggs.

Giant pandas live in high forests. They are shy and spend most of their time on their own. Their main food is a hard type of grass called bamboo, but they do eat other plants, too. These pandas sometimes climb trees, but usually live on the ground.

Animals of cold woods and forests

pine marten

red squirrel

brown bear

wild boar

badger

woodpecker

wolf

fox

41

Finding food

Red squirrels live in forests of
pine and fir trees. They eat nuts
and the scales and seeds from fir
cones. They also bury some nuts
and cones under the ground.
Then, in winter, when there are
no nuts or cones on the trees,
they dig them up again to eat.

Woodpeckers find their food in the forest, too. They use their hard, pointed beaks to make holes in the trees. Then they put their long, sticky tongues right into the holes. Small insects stick to their tongues and the woodpeckers quickly eat them.

Wild boars look for their food on the forest floor. They use their long noses to dig it up. Sometimes they find some of the cones and nuts hidden by squirrels. They also dig up fruit and small creatures like worms and insects.

Animals of grasslands and prairies

pronghorn

coyote

gopher

eagle

bison

prairie dog

kangaroo rat

45

Underground homes

The prairie dog is really a kind of squirrel. It lives underground with its family in a prairie dog "town". When the family goes above ground to find food, one prairie dog stands guard at the entrance to their tunnel.

Gophers also live in underground tunnels, but each gopher lives alone. A gopher's home has two tunnels, one underneath the other. The top tunnel is where the gopher finds roots and shoots to eat. The lower tunnel is where it lives and sleeps.

Animals of the deserts

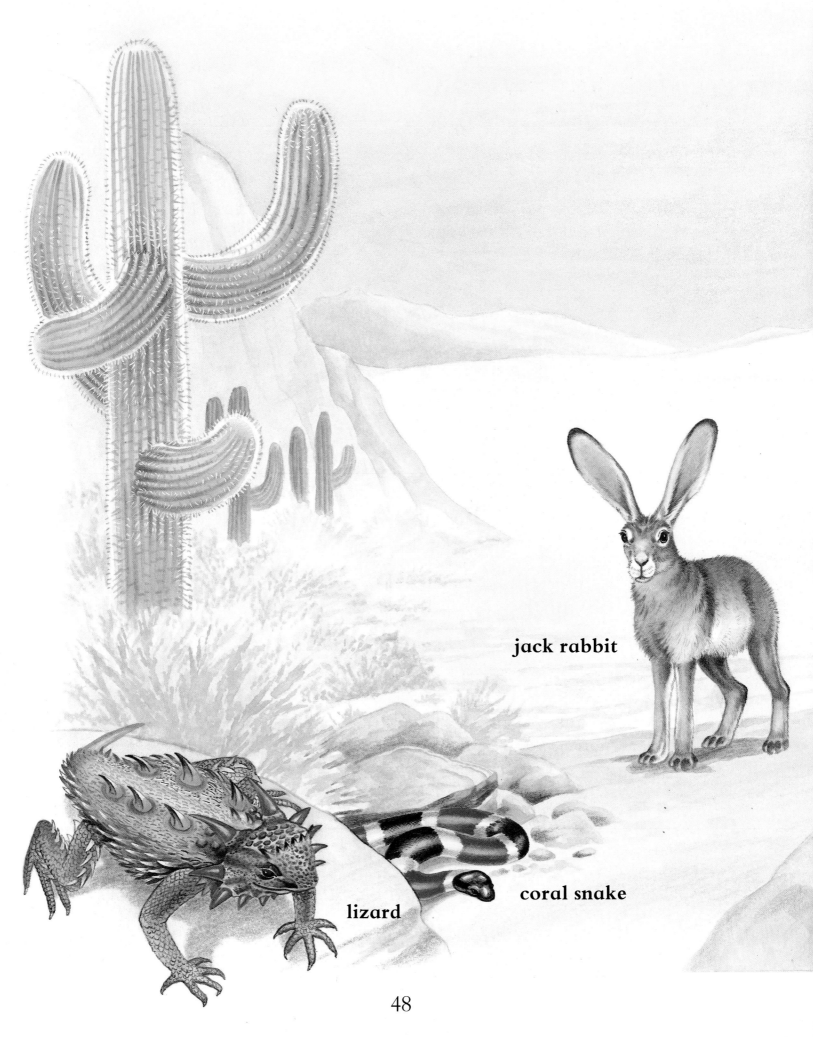

jack rabbit

lizard

coral snake

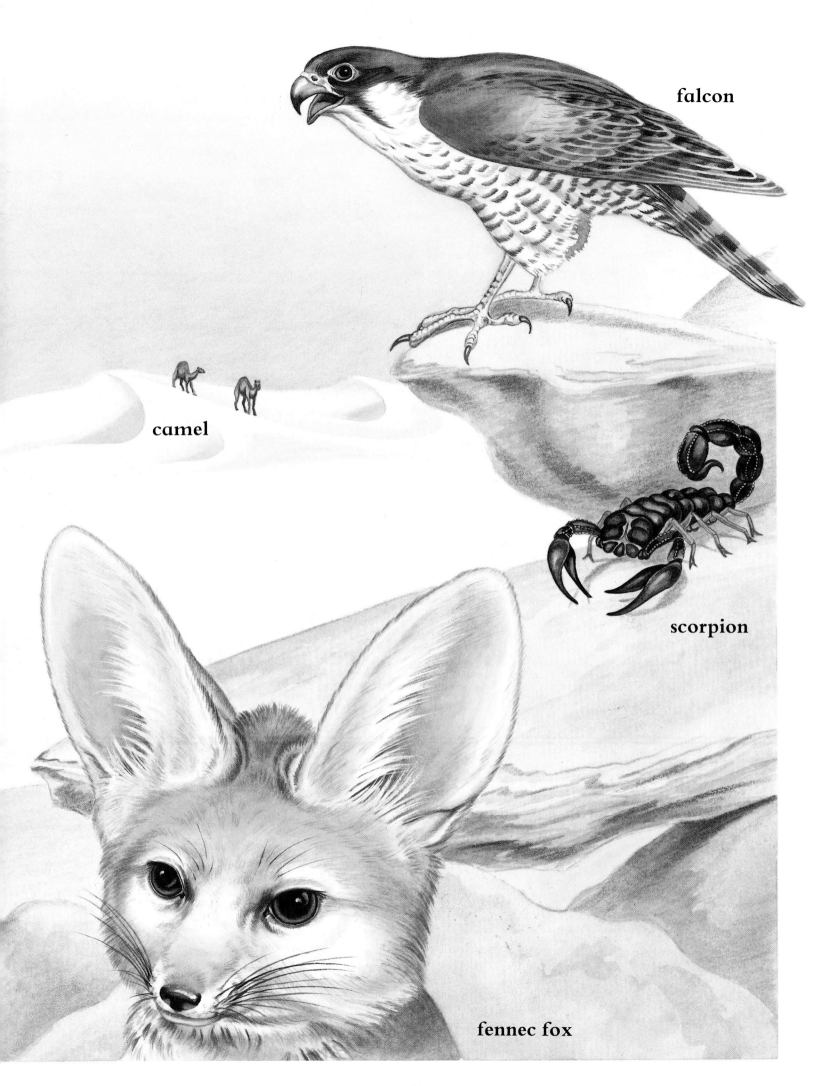

falcon

camel

scorpion

fennec fox

49

Camels

There are two types of camel. Arabian camels live in hot deserts. They have short hair so that they do not get too hot. Bactrian camels live in cold deserts. They have long hair to keep them warm.

All camels have lumps on their back called humps. Arabian camels have one hump and Bactrian camels have two humps. The humps have fat in them. The camels use this as food on their long journeys across the desert.

All camels also have special feet to help them walk in the desert. Each foot has two toes joined by a piece of skin. When a camel walks, the skin spreads out. This stops the camel from sinking in the sand.

Animals of the African plains

hippopotamus

African elephant

zebra

giraffe

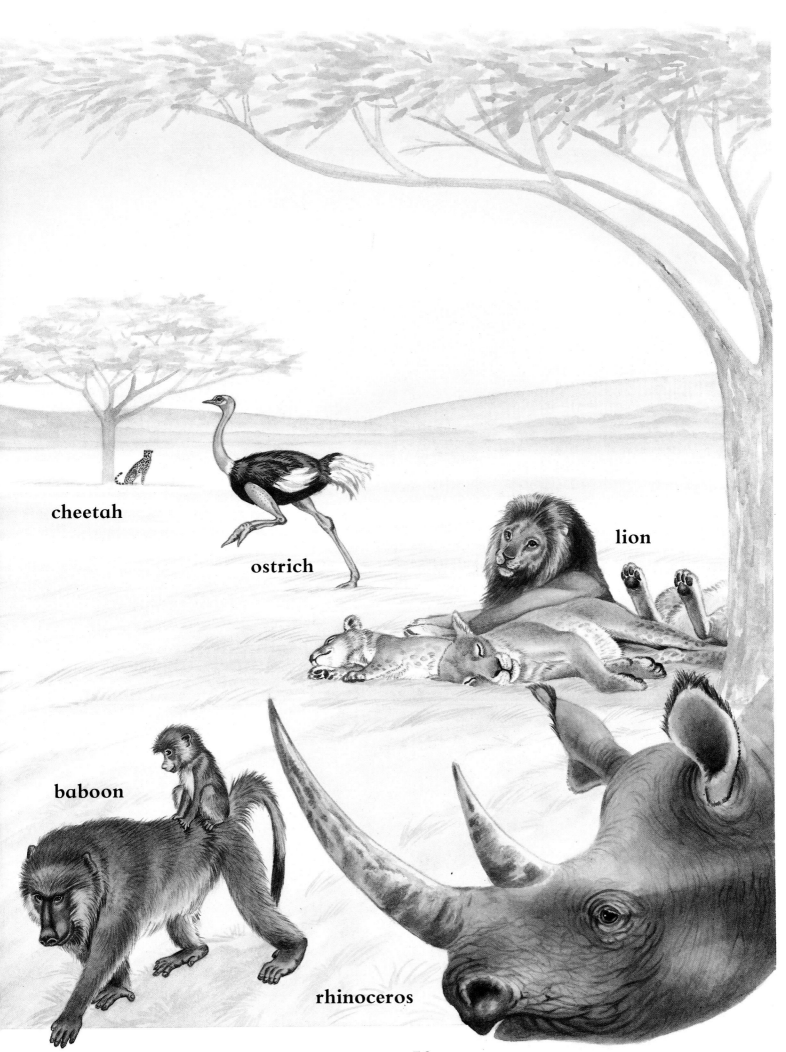

cheetah

ostrich

lion

baboon

rhinoceros

Biggest and fastest

Elephants are the biggest land animals in
the world. They roam around in family
groups called herds. Elephants live in hot
countries, so they need to keep cool. To do
this, they spray water over one another with
their trunks.

The cheetah can run faster than any other animal in the world. It needs to run fast to catch animals and birds to eat. Cheetahs hunt for their food early in the morning. They rest later in the day when the sun gets very hot.

Animals of the rainforests

monkey

leopard

tree frog

gorilla

bushbaby

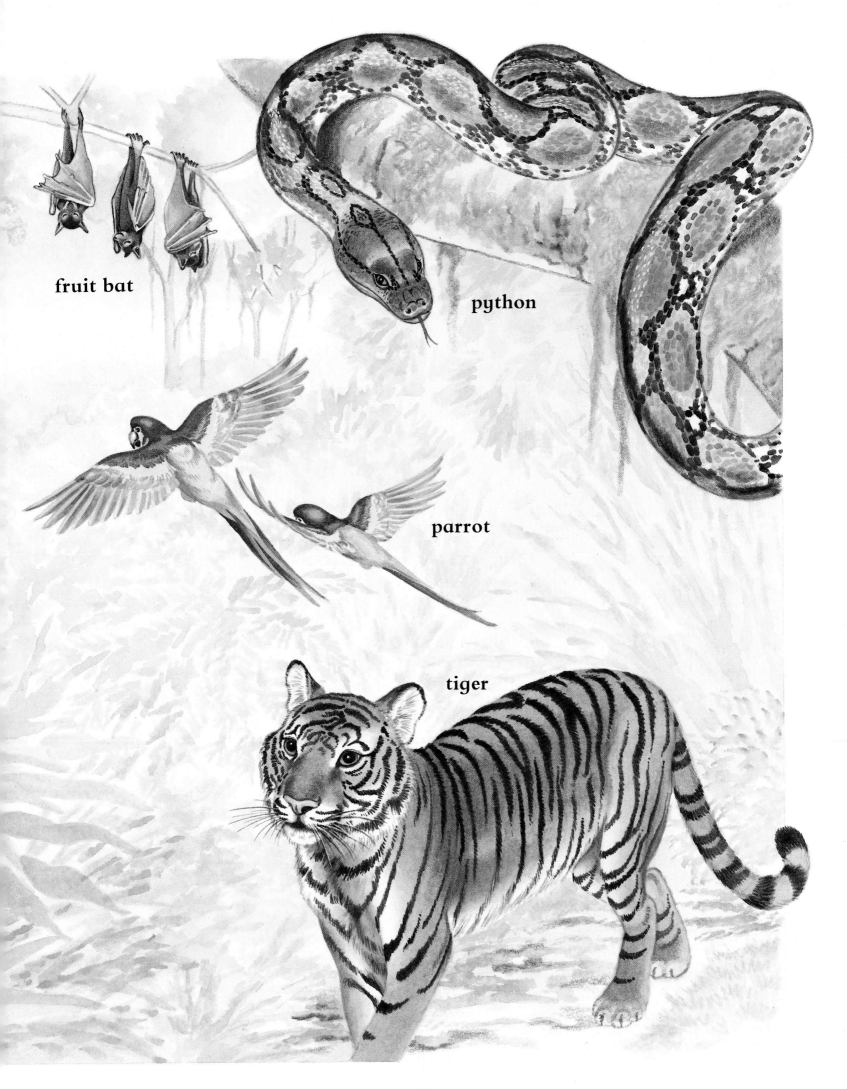

fruit bat

python

parrot

tiger

Rainforest animals at night

The leopard is a big, spotted cat. It is very good at climbing, running and swimming. In the daytime it sleeps quietly in the sun, usually in a tree. At night it hunts for food.

Fruit bats wake up when it starts to get dark. Then they fly off to find figs and other fruit to eat. In the morning they fly back to their tree. Then they hang upside down from a branch and go to sleep.

Bushbabies sleep in the daytime in their nests of leaves. At night they look for insects, small birds and fruit to eat. They have huge, round eyes to help them see in the dark.

59

Animals of Australia

wallaby

kangaroo

wombat

platypus

koala

kookaburra

echidna

Kangaroos

Kangaroos are strange animals. They have very long back legs and big, strong tails. Instead of walking, kangaroos jump along.

Baby kangaroos are called joeys. When a joey is born, it is only as big as a thumbnail. It does not have any fur and it cannot see. After it is born, it slowly crawls up to the pouch on the front of its mother's body. It stays inside the pouch for eight months, drinking milk and growing.

There are two main types of kangaroo. The red
kangaroo is big and lives on open ground. The grey
kangaroo is smaller and lives in forests.